To my mum, and all my
bird-watcher friends
who took me around

N. T.

magnificent
BIRDS

ILLUSTRATED BY NARISA TOGO

CANDLEWICK STUDIO
an imprint of Candlewick Press

Bald Eagle

Haliaeetus leucocephalus | NATIVE TO NORTH AMERICA

Spectacular flight displays are performed by the bald eagle both to defend territory and to reinforce a bond with their mate. A pair will swoop, soar, and cartwheel before locking talons and free-falling until they almost hit the earth. From its hunting grounds over lakes and coasts, the eagle returns to the same nest every year. Usually about 5 feet/1.5 meters wide and 4 feet/1.2 meters deep, the nests can grow much bigger as pairs add to them each year until the supporting branches snap under the increasing weight.

andean flamingo

Phoenicoparrus andinus | NATIVE TO SOUTH AMERICA

High up in the salt lakes of the Andes Mountains, huge flocks of pink Andean flamingos gather every summer to perform their courtship dance. Males march and shuffle in tight formation, turning their heads quickly from side to side in a movement known as flagging. They flick their neck back to preen their feathers and make jabbering and honking sounds. This striking display is designed to attract a mate; once a flamingo has a partner, they will stay together for several seasons and lay only one egg each year.

Flamingos' naturally gray plumage is transformed to bright pink by the food they eat. Andean flamingos can fly more than 700 miles/ 1,126 kilometers in a single day to find the right shallow, salty lake with the algae they prefer. All species of flamingos live in large flocks. The lesser flamingo, found in Africa, can gather in groups of more than a million birds. In addition to South America and Africa, species of flamingos are found in the Middle East and the Caribbean.

greater bird of paradise

Paradisaea apoda | NATIVE TO INDONESIA AND PAPUA NEW GUINEA

In the rain forests of Papua New Guinea, Indonesia, and Australia lives a family of birds with unusual plumage known collectively as birds of paradise. The males of the thirty-nine known species go to great lengths to attract a mate. Some, such as the Wilson's bird of paradise, show off bright primary colors on their feathers and skin. Others, such as the ribbon-tailed astrapia, have ornamental feathers that can be nearly 3 feet/1 meter long. Many birds of paradise inherit a sequence of dance steps they display to impress mates.

The greater bird of paradise is the largest of the family, at around 17 inches/ 43 centimeters in length. In the rain forest canopy, the male calls and waits for a female to enter its courting territory. Often another male will display alongside it in competition. Once a potential mate is watching, the bird will parade and hop back and forth, shaking and showing off the extravagant feathers on its back. It will then freeze in a pose, allowing the female to inspect its plume. Such displays can last for hours.

red-crowned crane

Grus japonensis | NATIVE TO CHINA, RUSSIA, KOREA, AND JAPAN

Named for the bare patch of colored skin on its head, the red-crowned crane, also known as the Japanese crane, is one of the rarest birds in the world. It is considered sacred and a symbol of luck and longevity in some parts of Asia. In Japan, it is known as *tanchōzuru*, and legends claim it can live 1,000 years. Red-crowned cranes usually mate for life and regularly perform a beautiful and elaborate dance with their partner to reinforce their bond. The pair will bow, throw their heads back, and leap into the air, flapping their long wings.

Though they roost in groups, the red-crowned crane tends to forage for fish, rice, and plants with its partner or family or alone. There are thought to be only 3,000 red-crowned cranes left in the world, as their wetland habitat dries up and fires destroy their nesting grounds.

common KINGFISHER

Alcedo atthis | NATIVE TO EURASIA AND NORTH AFRICA

A fast and efficient hunter, the kingfisher's success at snatching prey from the waterway where it lives is due to its ability to use two types of vision. Many birds have eyes on the sides of their head and therefore use monocular vision, whereby each eye works independently. Birds of prey tend to have eyes at the front and use binocular vision, which means both eyes work together. When the kingfisher dives, it switches from monocular vision in the air to binocular vision in the water. Using both allows it to judge the distance to its prey with deadly accuracy.

The kingfisher mostly eats small fish, but will swoop for aquatic insects and amphibians too. To sustain its whirring wingbeats and rapid flight, it needs to eat more than half its body weight each day. The kingfisher will leave its burrow in the riverbank to perch on a branch above the water. It waits until it spots movement below, then plunges after its prey in a characteristic flash of bright blue plumage.

toco toucan

Ramphastos toco | NATIVE TO SOUTH AMERICA

The toucan's large and colorful beak is instantly recognizable, but people have long been confused by what the bird uses it for. The beak can grow to nearly 8 inches/20 centimeters long, which can be almost a third of the toucan's body length. Made from keratin, the same protein as fingernails and hair, and filled with air pockets, the beak is surprisingly lightweight. It's unlikely the toucan uses its beak as a weapon. It has been observed using it to peel fruit and to play catch using scraps of food with a potential mate. It is also thought that the toucan can regulate its body temperature by adjusting how much blood reaches the beak's surface.

The toco is the largest of all toucans, and more than double the size of the smallest, the lettered araçari. Living in flocks of about six, toco toucans nest in the hollows of trees and are not very adept at flying, preferring to hop between branches. They lay between two and four eggs each year, and both parents stay to care for their young.

RUBY-THROATED HUMMINGBIRD

Archilochus colubris | NATIVE TO NORTH AND CENTRAL AMERICA

During courtship, the wings of the male ruby-throated hummingbird move faster than the wings of any other bird. As it displays to a female, the male hummingbird reaches an incredible two hundred wingbeats per second—nearly four times faster than its usual fifty-three beats. Hummingbird wings are connected to the body only at their shoulder joint, meaning they rotate in a similar way to insects' wings. No other bird has wings like this and it is why the hummingbird can hover and fly so acrobatically.

Such rapid movement means the hummingbird may eat twice its body weight in a day to maintain its energy. They use their long tongues to feed mainly on nectar and sap, but also eat insects and spiders. The hummingbird has one of the highest metabolic rates of any animal and a heart rate that can exceed 1,000 beats per minute. It builds a tiny, cupped nest out of grasses and spider webs, camouflaged with dead leaves, where the female cares for the offspring alone.

Bar-Tailed Godwit

Limosa lapponica | RANGES FROM THE ARCTIC TO AUSTRALIA AND NEW ZEALAND

The bar-tailed godwit makes the farthest nonstop flight of any bird. It takes a flock around eight days to fly more than 6,000 miles/11,000 kilometers over the vast Pacific Ocean from its breeding grounds in the Arctic to spend the winter in Australia and New Zealand. During the epic journey, the godwit burns through stores of body fat and loses more than half its body weight. Any organs unnecessary for the flight shrink in order to reduce the bird's weight and conserve energy. The godwit navigates by the sun and stars and rests by shutting down half its brain at a time.

When they return to the Arctic in the spring, the godwits take a longer coastal route and stop to feed at estuaries on the coast of the Yellow Sea to build up their fat reserves for the breeding season. The godwit will forage in marshes and mud flats for insects, worms, and crustaceans, competing with other members of the flock to store up enough energy for the rest of their relentless journey.

wandering albatross

Diomedea exulans | RANGES ACROSS SOUTHERN OCEAN AND NORTH PACIFIC

The wandering albatross has the largest wingspan of any modern bird species, measuring up to 12 feet/3.5 meters across. It spends most of its life in flight, primarily using a technique known as dynamic soaring to stay aloft. It glides up and down on ocean winds to generate momentum. In this way the albatross can be in the air for hours and travel vast distances without once flapping its wings. An albatross can cover more than 10,000 miles/16,000 kilometers in a single journey. Some have been known to circumnavigate the globe in only forty-six days.

The wandering albatross sometimes follows ships for food and holds a deep-rooted place in maritime lore as a symbol of good luck. The albatross only comes ashore to breed on remote islands. Pairs mate for life and take turns caring for a single egg each year. Once a young albatross has its flight plumage, which develops before it is a year old, it spends the next five to ten years at sea until it is ready to mate. Thought to be able to live for up to fifty years, the wandering albatross is one of the few birds that usually dies of old age, although modern fishing techniques are an increasing threat to its longevity.

AUSTRALIAN PELICAN

Pelecanus conspicillatus | NATIVE TO AUSTRALIA, NEW GUINEA, AND INDONESIA

The Australian pelican's eye-catching bill is the longest of any bird's. It measures around 19 inches/50 centimeters, and the elastic throat pouch that hangs from it can stretch to hold as much as 3 gallons/11 liters of water, though it is not used to store food or liquid. Instead, it is an effective and sensitive tool for catching fish in murky water. Once a fish is scooped into the pouch, the pelican presses its bill to its chest to drain the water, then swallows its catch whole. Often Australian pelicans will hunt in large groups, sometimes of more than 1,000 birds.

Though big and heavy, the Australian pelican is very buoyant, thanks to air sacs under its skin and in its bones. Like other large birds, it soars on thermal air currents rather than flapping its long wings when flying, which allows it to cover great distances easily. Pelicans nest in flocks on wetlands and waterways. Each female lays two or three eggs in shallow bowls in earth or sand, but the nest can be a brutal place for the young. The first-hatched chick is often the only one to survive; usually the largest, it is given the most food by its parents and may kill its siblings.

barn owl

Tyto alba | WORLDWIDE

The near-silent night flights of the barn owl are not the only thing that makes it such
a deadly hunter. Its sense of hearing is among the most sensitive of any animal.
Although it hunts mainly at dawn and dusk, the barn owl is able to catch prey in total
darkness from sound alone. Its heart-shaped face collects sound, and its asymmetrical
ear placement allows the owl to determine prey's location with pinpoint accuracy.
With its large eyes, the barn owl's vision is twice as sensitive as a human's.

The barn owl swallows prey whole, then regurgitates inedible materials, like fur
and bone, in a compact pellet. Owls mate for life and raise young together. The male
owl brings food back to be shared among its owlets. At ten weeks, young
barn owls have mastered flying and begin to hunt. Despite this parental care, as
many as three-quarters of barn owls die in their first year. Nearly half of hatchlings
never make it out of the nest, most commonly because of food shortage.

emperor penguin

Aptenodytes forsteri | NATIVE TO ANTARCTICA

In the frozen Antarctic, where the temperature can drop to -70°F/-60°C, extraordinary parenting is needed to keep emperor penguin chicks alive. Once the female has laid her egg, she passes it off to the male and leaves to hunt in the ocean. She may travel long distances to reach her ocean hunting grounds. There she will dive deeper than any other bird—more than 1,800 feet/500 meters—to catch fish, krill, and squid.

While she is away, the male balances the egg on his feet, protecting it from the elements under a brood pouch and huddling with other penguins to conserve heat. For two months, the male eats nothing, and may lose almost half his body weight. When the chick hatches, its father produces a kind of milk from his esophagus to feed it. When the female returns, she regurgitates food for the chick and takes over its care, leaving the male free to hunt. Once the chick is old enough to survive outside the brood pouch, it joins a crèche of up to several thousand other juveniles. Eventually the whole colony will trek to the ocean together.

kakapo

Strigops habroptila | NATIVE TO NEW ZEALAND

The kakapo has been in New Zealand since prehistoric times and can live up to ninety years, but despite this, it is one of the world's rarest birds. Kakapos are found only on three small islands in the Pacific Ocean. By the 1970s, introduced predators like feral cats had decimated the population. Only eighteen male kakapos were thought to be left in the world. The species looked doomed to extinction until a small population of both males and females was discovered and an intensive conservation program began. The kakapos were moved to protected islands, where they were supplied with food and closely monitored. Through this painstaking work, the kakapo population has now reached more than 100 individuals.

The kakapo is a large parrot that climbs instead of flies. It only emerges from its nest on the ground at night. The kakapo is also the only parrot to have a "lek" breeding system, where groups of males gather to compete for females. The male digs a bowl on high ground to act as an amplifier. Then, using its thoracic sac, it inflates like a balloon and makes a sonic boom that can be heard from up to 3 miles/5 kilometers away. It can perform like this for eight hours without a break, interspersing its booms with high-frequency *ching* sounds that pinpoint its location to any interested female.

peregrine falcon

Falco peregrinus | WIDESPREAD

The peregrine falcon is the fastest animal in the world. It reaches speeds of more than 240 miles/300 kilometers per hour when diving for prey. This movement is known as a stoop. The falcon achieves this incredible speed by virtue of its powerful flight muscles and by being efficiently streamlined. Its pointed wings and stiff feathers cut through the air with little resistance. It breathes at twice the speed of other birds because of special bones that divert air away from its nostrils and keep air pressure at a safe level.

Fittingly, "peregrine" comes from the Latin for "wanderer," as it is found all over the world. Recently it has become a more common sight in cities, drawn by skyscrapers that mimic the cliff faces where the peregrine usually nests and an abundance of prey such as pigeons. On cliffs and buildings, young falcons are raised in shallow bowls scratched into dirt. Generations of falcons often use the same nesting sites for hundreds of years.

NARISA TOGO is a printmaker and illustrator with a lifelong love of birds. After receiving a BS in ecology from the Tokyo University of Agriculture and Technology, she completed an MA in children's book illustration at the Cambridge School of Art. When she is not in her studio producing the intricate reduction linocut artwork featured in *Magnificent Birds*, Narisa Togo takes groups bird-watching. She lives in Japan.

THE ROYAL SOCIETY for the **PROTECTION OF BIRDS** is the largest nature conservation charity in Britain. Formed over 120 years ago, the RSPB works to provide a home for nature and protect species from decline. It has more than a million members. The publishers are grateful for their consultation on this project.

Text copyright © 2017 by Walker Books Ltd
Illustrations copyright © 2017 by Narisa Togo

First U.S. edition 2018

Library of Congress Catalog Card Number pending
ISBN 978-1-5362-0169-7

18 19 20 21 22 23 CCP 10 9 8 7 6 5 4 3 2 1

Printed in Shenzhen, Guangdong, China

This book was typeset in Avenir Next.
The illustrations were done in linocut.

Candlewick Studio
an imprint of
Candlewick Press
99 Dover Street
Somerville, Massachusetts 02144

www.candlewickstudio.com